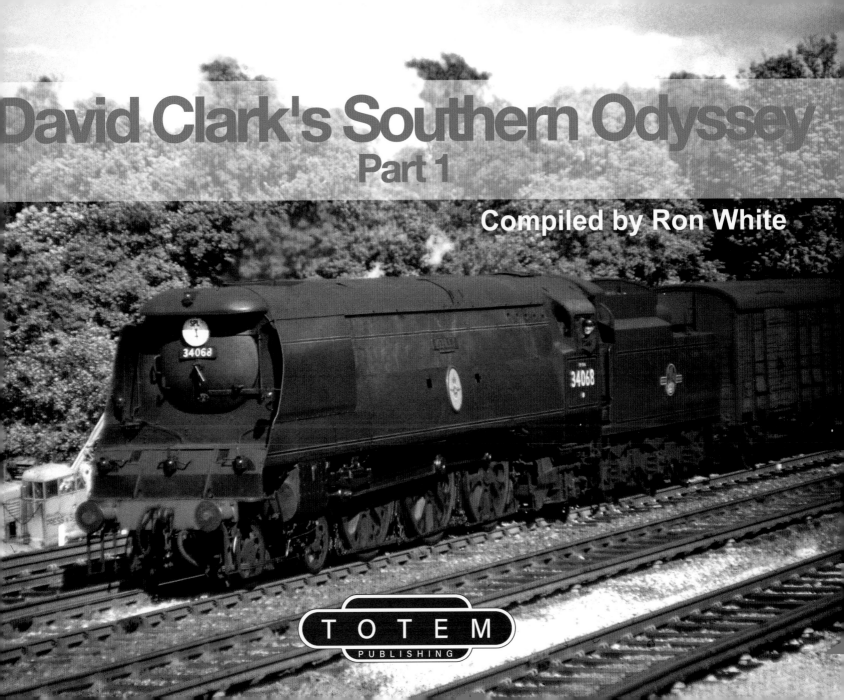

David Clark's Southern Odyssey
Part 1

Compiled by Ron White

34068

34068

TOTEM
PUBLISHING

© Images and Design: The Transport Treasury 2022. Text: Ron White

ISBN 978-1-913893-26-2

First published in 2022 by Transport Treasury Publishing Ltd. 16 Highworth Close, High Wycombe, HP13 7PJ
Totem Publishing, an imprint of Transport Treasury Publishing.

www.ttpublishing.co.uk

Printed in Tarxien, Malta By Gutenberg Press Ltd.

'David Clark's Southern Odyssey: Part 1' is one of a series of books on specialist transport subjects published in strictly limited numbers and produced under the Totem Publishing imprint using material only available at The Transport Treasury.

Front Cover: BB 34067 *Tangmere* on a down boat train at Downsbridge Road, on the Catford loop. This was Ken Wightman's preferred area and I thought it must be his shot, but the mount bears all David's cryptic notes so there we are - a mystery to start with, the only shot he took there, the only picture taken on that date, but too good not to use. *18.10.1960*

Vignette: the man himself, neat, calm, respectable - the apotheosis of accountancy - could you imagine him as a member of the Master Neverers Association driving a clapped out car to the public danger and sleeping in freezing PW huts in the Cheviots? No, me neither.

Frontispiece: 34068 *Kenley* clears the Cray valley with an up boat train from Dover via Chatham; all the really heavy work was over in the first climb to Shepherdswell, waiting for the prepared fire of briquettes to burn through before getting any more into the box; black coal on black coal = 160 lbs of smoke and no steam! *7.6.1959*

Introduction
DAVID BARRY CLARK - 1936-2014

When our publisher said that he MIGHT be able to get hold of David's slides I was seized with a fine enthusiasm for I had been allowed to use some of his output in the Colour-Rail catalogue from 2008 onwards and knew it to be technically good if regionally restricted; and I knew he held the late Ken Wightman's slides which went back well into the 1950s when few of us could afford black & white film, let alone think of colour or 35mm for that matter. By then I had got up to a folding Kodak Autograph camera using 116 size film and it wasn't until 1959 I could afford an Agfa Isolette, which did have a decent lens, and a Kodak Retinette 1B (which didn't unless stopped right down and I only found that out after I bought it).

David's sister agreed to sell the slides if a book could be put together as a memorial to her brother whom she hardly knew as he was 12 years her senior - I offered since I was senior to him and had lived through those times and I already had a toe in the door with an insight into what might be possible. I knew Capital Transport had used plenty of his slides in their excellent series of books now long out of print (I remember them, but my library went when we downsized in 2011 and how I miss it).

And so, the slides duly arrived, two plastic boxes containing…? NOT what I expected, hundreds of slides jammed together filed in locomotive classes, virtually no Western/Midland, a smidgeon of Eastern/Scottish but enough slides taken within five miles of home to fill TWO books - I was clearly going to have an interesting time in sorting the sheep from the sheep let alone finding a passing goat of no fixed abode. We have our methods Watson, and this volume covers the early years when everything had to be done by bicycle or by using LT buses on Routes 61 or 161A (good old RTs from Bromley Common depot) and we end nearly at Dover covering most of that line but not touching the Chatham/Ramsgate area - what he didn't do is every bit as fascinating as what he managed to do on weekends only, using only 20 exposure cassettes, couldn't afford 36s, occasionally sliding into b/w positives (wonderfully sharp) or early Agfa (wonderfully blunt and largely ignored herein).

Although he took his first slide in 1953, his output was very small and it wasn't until 1959 that he put academia (St. Olave's, no less) and evening classes (remember them?) behind him. By then he had gained whatever qualifications he needed to start in accountancy with Allied Suppliers and he stayed with them until retirement by which time they were part of the Morrison Group. Nowadays no-one is encouraged to stick around, but then we were "Company Men" and proud to be so, working in my case, two Saturdays out of three, out of which three hours travelling wrecked my leisure time - he spent far less time getting back to New Eltham and could get to St. Mary Cray Junction in no time flat.

I haven't been able to trace much of his formative years, he seems to have missed National Service because of asthma, he never married, remaining in the family home after his parents died and his sister married and went away. Bachelor status enabled him to buy a car (a RED Austin A40 which he kept forever), then a blue Triumph Dolomite, then a Honda, but no-one seems to be able to remember which model, but that, too, was kept until he died and the two elderly hulks went to enthusiasts for rebuilding.

David's final years were dogged with health problems and he went under protest into a nursing home nearer his sister; within earshot of the Basingstoke - Reading line, where he died in 2014. The slides went to Rodney Lissenden for safekeeping and he made them available to publishers but this is the first attempt to make something logical and chronological from the collection - if some have appeared elsewhere, I apologise and I'm sure other publishers are sitting on others in the hope that they may have been forgotten.

Ron White
Chesham, October 2022

(1) E1 31545 has an up Ramsgate in the same area, within cycle range of home; David was still only 20, some 15 years younger than the fiery E1 which had plenty of life left in her. *8.1956*

(2) MN 35021 *New Zealand Line* is looking a bit scruffy - I can't remember when she was rebuilt and I don't really associate her with the Eastern Section, but here she is for you on another boat train via Chatham; drooping reporting number. *8.1956*

(3) BB 34070 *Manston* appears to be going to the coast via Maidstone East if that head code (and my memory) tells the truth. *4.1957*

(4) U1 31904 comes up from Ramsgate with a semi-fast; some said under-boilered, some said over-cylindered but they gave 35 years dogged service especially if you knew their little ways. *4.4.1959*

(5) N 31413 passing David's home station at New Eltham, going I know not where or by what route. I've forgotten that head code if I ever knew it; I can't ever remember seeing even a b/w shot of steam on that line and I missed this one on the first trawl through! *2.5.1959*

(6) D1 31145 going down to Dover via Chatham, not a care in the world for her - a snip compared with a documented wartime job when (substituting for a sick U class) she was given 14 packed coaches to get from Canonbury to Basingstoke over the sharp grades of the LMS electrified line via Hampstead - with a good push-off and a clear run she did it: 500 tons behind a 4-4-0 (and LMS 2Ps had to be banked up the Lickey on more than 4 coaches!). *16.5.1959*

(7) WC 34016 *Bodmin* is seen broadside close by one of those handy footbridges which so helped the young photographer to hone his craft - I think this is for Folkestone but that's guesswork. *16.5.1959*

(8) V 30939 *Leatherhead* is for Ramsgate and is climbing that nasty bit of 1 in 95 out of Bromley South up to Bickley - this one has been attacked by Bulleid and given a wide chimney and Lemaitre exhaust but the originals were just as good (and prettier). I think those tall chimneys are at Bromley Gasworks which once had rail access for coal deliveries. *16.5.1959*

(9) N15 30769 *Sir Balan* was one of Stewarts Lane's favourite Arthurs (with 30768 *Sir Balin*) and looks as if he has had a hard week's work and not enough polishing - Ramsgate certainly won't do it for them. This must have been Whit-Saturday and a very good time to make a proper start at your chosen hobby. *16.5.1959*

(10) BB 34071 *601 Squadron* with another boat train via Chatham; two GUVs on the front give the game away and the untidy background shows work is still in progress. *18.5.1959*

(11) N 31405 shuffles towards the Chislehurst Loop and will probably end up in the yards between Grove Park and Ivver Green (to many: Hither Green to us). The Ns were saddled with the unlikely and untranslatable nickname of "Mongolipers" and if any passing centenarian can come up with its origin I'd love to know. *18.5.1959*

(12) WC 34005 *Barnstaple* is fast for Folkestone & Dover via Orpington and Tonbridge. No GUVs, no boat connection. *23. 5. 1959*

(13) N 31810 will proceed in a statesmanlike manner towards Ramsgate; not a lot to choose between her and 31405 save the tender. *23.5.1959*

(14) BB 34066 *Spitfire* on yet another up boat train - now, will he go via Penge (always pronounced Ponge by Terry Wogan!) or will the driver if "good with a pencil", as the phrase was, claim he came up via the Catford Loop, a mile or two longer and worth a few coppers in the pay packet - risky but some got away with it! *23.5.1959*

(15) V 30925 *Cheltenham* on a down Ramsgate, hard to believe this sad specimen was the masthead/ flagship of the RCTS. *24.5.1959*

(16) E1 31545 leads a disreputable BB 34073 *249 Squadron* on the "up Blue" - the Night Ferry with SNCF stock and this was a really heavy job for a BB and so a fiery particle was tacked on; if the BB slipped the E1 didn't and the job was done. *4.6.1959*

Left: (17) U1 31892 is a credit to Faversham shed as she rolls downhill into Bromley South station with an up Ramsgate; all Moguls were notorious mud throwers and were normally light brown all over. *7.6.1959*

Opposite: (18) BB 34078 *222 Squadron* tiptoes through the redesigned layout - this is a bit short of colour but it does show the old layout tipping down the cutting side, speed restricted and a pain in the neck. *7.6.1959*

(19) N15 30793 *Sir Ontzlake* has had the front buffer beam repainted after a minor nudge somewhere; quietly done on shed without having to answer silly questions. David used his bicycle well to get back to the junction! *7.6.1959*

(20) U1 31895 - see what I mean about the livery? And you have a choice of duty numbers with 121 added by a failed Boy Scout as she drops into Bromley South after depopulating Ramsgate. *13.6.1959*

(21) N15 30803 *Sir Harry Le Fise Lake* (splendid name!) had a small tender and was a little hamstrung, thereby needing to put the bag in at some convenient column on the way to or from the coast; probably Faversham/Chatham on this job. Faversham was favoured as the adjoining pub would have two pints drawn for drivers who blew their code on approach - eight minutes to tie the Dover/Ramsgate parts together, ideal! *13.6.1959*

(22) V 30938 *St. Olave's* was appropriately his last shot before Phase One of the Kent Coast Modification Scheme kicked in and he would have to transfer his attentions to further south but still within cycle or bus reach of home. A final down Ramsgate at St Mary Cray Junction on 13.6.1959 ends this section but there was a pocket of steam beyond Swanley which would have to wait the arrival of a red Austin A40. *13.6.1959*

(23) The Southern Railway had always fretted about North Kent's north facing and empty shoreline and thought it might be made productive by creating holiday resorts of an initially primitive nature, something pre-Butlins, a camping site with a pub, cheap but not necessarily cheerful and Allhallows-on-Sea (?) received a branch line from Gravesend in 1929. Almost as soon as he had got his driving licence he investigated; at Sharnal Street he stood off and put the train into the scenery (while there still was some) and H 31305 goes north-east. *22.5.1961*

(24) 31716 on her way back to Gravesend, how sensible to show the whole station area rather than a close-up of the loco, efficient and pretty little thing though it was. *30.9.1961*

(25) H 31518 at the terminus, a long stark island platform, with little visible beyond, naught for your comfort. *30.9.1961*

(26) C 31716 would have had the branch freight, had there been any, but has to settle for a tankful of dubious fluid. *30.9.1961*

(27) H 31308 reveals the scenic glory of the Isle of Grain, two man-made objects to savour; the Costa del Sol it never could have been and this final miserable shot is close to closure of the passenger service. *29.10.1961*

(28) H 31305 at Middle Stoke where the line to Grain and Port Victoria went eastwards. What a seething scene of activity, maybe the Good Doctor did get one or two correct. *20.9.1961*

(29) BB 34066 *Spitfire* comes down towards Petts Wood Junction - I judge this to be the first colour shot he ever took and I date it as 1953 - there is nothing at all on the mount but geriatric forensic skills have been brought to bear on the slide. It might be the Kentish Belle (half Pullman, half standard stock), the Maunsell four-set in blood & custard is fading away.

(30) V 30909 *St. Paul's* has a down Hastings passing a nice tall semaphore which won't have long to live. *2.4.1956*

(31) BB 34067 *Tangmere* on a down Dover showing the lines to Bickley and the massive poles needed by the Signalling Department. *1956*

(32) C 31268 runs towards Orpington and an unknown destination, this reliable old dear makes a change from a welter of Bulleids. *2.1957*

(33) Standard 5 73089 hasn't yet received her nameplates and must be fairly new. I think this is an up Ramsgate via Ashford but...? *4.1958*

(34) V 30935 *Sevenoaks* will get through those tiny tunnels of the Hastings line without scraping the sides, but the canted side-sheets will make life a misery for any fully grown footplate men. *4.1958*

Opposite: (35) 7MT 70004 *William Shakespeare* on the down Arrow just before transfer away with 70014 *Iron Duke*. Much loved by the heavy-handed men, they would take a pounding, steam freely and fly over the ground, but they were hard-riding compared with a Bulleid. *4.1958*

Right: (36) MN 35001 *Channel Packet* winds through those same curves on a miserable day, but this gave David plenty of exhaust; she looks rough and must be due for rebuilding after which she won't reappear here. In 1941 she, and her sisters, were known as *Flannel Jackets*, mercifully not forever. *2.5.1959*

(37) MN 35028 *Clan Line* looks a treat after emerging from Eastleigh in green and really was a new machine. When blue both she and 35027 were iffy, but were transformed. *13.6.1959*

(38) BB 34087 *145 Squadron* still has her original tender which looked nicer but kept her off the really heavy jobs to and from Dover. It must have been somewhere here that David met, not Goliath, but one Ken Smith, some years his junior and living in Orpington; also, with knowledge of the unsurfaced tracks in the woods, a sturdy bicycle AND binoculars to look far north for anything interesting creeping round the Chislehurst Loop to St. Mary Cray. Tally-ho! and away we go, increasing output for the day. Ken is still around, a bit fragile but full of memories and I'll be leaning on him for help when needed. *13.6.1959*

(39) BB 34089 *602 Squadron* on an up boat train near Petts Wood, this was always a good one and after rebuilding went to Salisbury. *19.7.1959*

(40) BB 34078 *222 Squadron* has a down Dover quietly under control approaching Petts Wood; David is creeping slowly south under Ken's influence, and still dreaming of a car! *7.9.1959*

(41) WC 34026 *Yes Tor* on another one, with another faded three-set leading but these are Mark Ones - was the weather that good all the time? Oh, and look at the adjoining white house whose chimney flues will ensure a warm garden but a cold house. *9.9.1959*

(42) L1 31756 on what seems to be a down engineers' train by an armless semaphore; these were known as German Glasshouses although they had nothing Teutonic about them; they were a marked improvement on the Ls (some of which were built by Borsig of Berlin) and a side-window cab (a very small glasshouse, standing room only). *9.9.1959*

(43) BB 34077 *603 Squadron* gets a spoonful at just the right moment; her Mark Ones haven't had time to fade and a solitary roof board isn't a lot of help and I'm sure there's a dirty disc in front of the chimney to aid the signalman. *9.9.1959*

(44) D1 31739 on a down stopper at Petts Wood Junction - this shot shows the extent of the earthworks needed, we never heard a peep out of the environmentalists in those days. This might be the 07.24 to Ramsgate but the slide doesn't say. *18.6.1960*

(45) BB 34089 *602 Squadron* on the down Arrow - in those days engines were so reliable they kept turning up day after day on specific jobs. But the Arrow demanded engines with all the special fitments for the trimmings (especially those monster wooden arrows!). *18.6.1960*

(46) E1 31497 on the wondrous 07.24 London Bridge - Ramsgate, calling, it seemed, at all stations, halts, signals, the odd PW hut, an amazing survival. Only just enough light for a sufficiently short exposure to stop her dead. K1 was originally ASA8, then 10 and K2 was ASA25. And another piece of useless information, this loco carried a chimney originally carried by a 2-6-4T which was converted to a Mogul after a serious crash a century ago. *22.7.1960*

(47) N1 31880 has a freight of caravan length coming down to Petts Wood Junction, stormy sky sets off the clean exhaust. *16.10.1960*

(48) Turn through 90 degrees and the result is entirely different, trees instead of new earthworks, backlit steam, already David has absorbed some of what slow colour film can (and can't) do, and that trains in the scenery have just as much to offer as record shots (though we need both). *16.10.1960*

Top: (49) WC 34027 *Taw Valley* on the down Man of Kent, one of the last trains to carry a headboard, and for the rake to be roof boarded; this last refinement remaining simply because the platforming at Charing Cross did not enable the staff to remove the boards before the return working was due out and it was easier to leave them on and keep the title. There never was a "Kentish Man" to celebrate that particular group and I'm sure Frank Muir (who was one) would have found suitable words to remedy the deficiency had he been a railway enthusiast. *7.9.1959*

Approaching Orpington we have got beyond the range of the 161A which terminated at Petts Wood station but the 61 went through Orpington and ended up, I think, at Farnborough and it ends the period of saturation coverage for which we might not be grateful - but we should when it reveals a lot of what the railways got on with - major surgery without interruption to the service, lifted loop lines with speed restrictions, five miles of quadrupling the tracks, eliminating flat junctions - look closely at these pictures and see how many odd bits of points are visible but disconnected, all done by an army of men overnight and at weekends with great chunks of track having been pre-assembled at distant New Cross Gate and brought in as required - maybe picture 42 is a bit of it. Oh, and I don't remember the papers being full of hairy protesters, nor even NIMBYS, and when the job was eventually finished, it looked a treat, try that shallow-angled cutting side with the fresh brick drainage channels. And a final thought, although the pictures are spread over several weekends, they could have been done in one, such was the volume of traffic in those days - much of it hauled by 4-4-0s!

One of the troubles of a short main line is that the same engines can be seen four times in a day with two different sets of men; eight hours for them which normally meant an out and back plus some filling-in turns which were always available. Stewarts Lane allocated engines to jobs as far as possible, starting with the down Arrow and the Blue getting priority, then the boat trains. I've tried for variety but not always succeeded, tried to avoid specials, which everyone hammered. David will shortly get his A40 and expand his horizons but not until we've cleared Orpington.

Bottom: (50) N 31406 brings down vans under the lovely gantry by the electric car sheds, only one off so a halt seems probable. *3.7.1960*

(51) BB 34089 *602 Squadron* is inbound and looking in need of TLC. I can only see a brake van behind the tender but the originals were not loved on freight despite OVS craftily calling them mixed traffic locos. Orpington had a control centre and the loco inspectors had a hutch there so it behoved everyone to behave when passing through. *8.9.1959*

(52) WC 34004 *Yeovil* brings an up Dover past Orpington. A box, well elevated to give sightlines over the bridge; there's another such affair at Paddock Wood where the Hawkhurst branch trains ran underneath, but no photograph taken. This more or less colourless shot was taken on Agfa, he tried three reels but gave up and went back to K2/25. *30.6.1960*

(53) V 30929 *Malvern* is out of sight of authority and can get stuck into the climb to Chelsfield tunnel, note the new rail dropped ready for action; another mixed rake for Folkestone. *5.8.1960*

(54) WC 34100 *Appledore* has got through the tunnel with the down Arrow and clears the last few yards towards Knockholt station and the summit - she became a favourite for the job. *14.5.1961*

Top: (55) V 30932 *Blundells* comes up to Polhill tunnel passing Polhill Intermediate's down signals, never easy to spot early if the tunnel was full of smoke. For years 30932 was paired with the unique high-sided tender but Ashford had a fit of the vapours one day and painted it black instead of green and so 30905 got it instead and her unexpectedly green one went to 30932 - couldn't have happened to nicer people. *4.8.1960*

Bottom: (56) H 31530 waits at Dunton Green with the connection for Westerham, another delightful little line doomed to be flattened by concrete as the M25 demanded its trackbed - as usual the final specials were packed and hauled by strange locomotives, but this is what it was really like. *8.10.1961*

(57) H 31530 near Chevening Halt; for me as lovely a picture as David ever took - on the final day he took another with an H with the Union Flag across the smokebox door and woolly skulls hanging over the side but how could that be given preference over this classic tree and the train put in its place? *14.10.1961*

(58) H 31530 has got the full length of the branch and now leans gracefully against the platform edge at Westerham - the bicycle under the canopy is the only sign that anyone lived here and loved it. *8.10.1961*

(59) H 31530 leaves for Dunton Green passing the box; the line had all the trimmings but needed more passengers, pity the admirable pub across the road couldn't get in the shot as well. *8.10.1961*

(60) V 30935 *Sevenoaks* approaches HER station with a down Hastings, the line from Bat and Ball can just be seen coming in. *7.1956*

Top: (61) D1 31749/E1 31067 make their final appearance on stage clean, comely, and waiting for a train, which will, after due applause, turn out to be a ballast working at Bat & Ball which they will convey to Ashford and be withdrawn after 40 years of good reliable work. Either would have looked good in the National Collection but I suppose I have to admit that an original Coppertop D 737 looks even better, especially in that glorious livery. 4.10.1961

Bottom: (62) After leaving Tubs Hill, down trains had the pleasure of tipping over the summit and cascading down through the tunnel which could well be full of smoke from an up train - if it was and the first thing you saw was Weald Intermediate's distant ON, then life was full of action, a full application and hope for the best as it was a shortish block. Drivers had been known to put the gear in reverse to help, but not on an unrebuilt BB/WC/MN (because no-one could guess what might happen inside the sump amidst all those chains, gears and 65 gallons of hot oil). One day, in a flap, with a VIP (and the Guv'nor!) on the footplate, one of the old lags in the Boat Gang did, but they all lived happily ever afterwards, but it never happened again, as far as I know, but what it did to the works was never revealed. Then sedately on down to Hildenborough station where H 31263 is leaving on a golden evening aiming at Tonbridge but the head code argues she will go through to Tunbridge Wells West. 28.10.1961

(63) L 31771 is in the locomotive sidings by Tonbridge station; although known as a German, I think she was Mancunian. Another colourless Agfa (you won't get any more), may I draw your attention to the factory - you won't find many of them around the country. *2.4.1960*

(64) Working west we'll eventually hit the Central Section, but Penshurst is Eastern, and N 31869 has steam to spare as she trundles towards Redhill. *1.6.1963*

(65) U1 31902 at Bough Beech (how very Garden of England!), aiming at Redhill and a good chance of being accurate. *14.5.1960*

(66) **U1 31901 is east of Edenbridge (good title for a novel?) and enjoys the scenery, one coach per cylinder is uneconomic.** *21.6.1960*

Top: (67) N 31868 leaves Edenbridge with a freight for Redhill and subsequent redistribution, the battered mineral wagon could quietly drop into a preserved Great Central windcutter and be welcomed. Somewhere along this stretch was one of the oddest crossings you could hardly see, where this line, in the bottom of a cutting, found itself on a bridge going over the Oxted - Uckfield route which was in Little Browns tunnel, which had to be opened out and the gap surrounded by paling fences! You could get a shot of something on the bridge, but not of anything underneath - and as that line was Central Division we'll go back to Tonbridge and proceed eastwards. *13.4.1963*

Bottom: (68) H 31193 leaves Tonbridge and will end up at Maidstone West (I think); the wagons hold good bright loco coal, Tonbridge shed was lucky to avoid Tilmanstone Antiglow, as it was known. *4.8.1960*

(69) E1 31019 has a short ballast and has been looped at Paddock Wood to allow something to overtake, try inching forward with 6" 9" wheels and plenty of steam, not easy. *22.4.1961*

(70) WC 34100 *Appledore* in full flight just east of Paddock Wood station, the line to Maidstone goes off to the right, and the Hawkhurst branch runs under the signal box, but not for much longer. *2.6.1961*

(71) H 31177 at Horsmonden bears neither head code nor lamp but is coming down to Paddock Wood - I'm sure this one has been seen before but the shot does include an oast house AND reveals there was no passing loop here so there is historical merit in this one. *2.6.1961*

(72) H 31177 pushes off towards Hawkhurst from Goudhurst's fine station building, the hutch on the up side wasn't comparable - another shot in the last few days of the branch, a pity the loco is such a ratty specimen. *2.6.1961*

David never got to Hawkhurst (neither, for that matter, did the railway) for although the station said it was, it wasn't, and you had to be stern of purpose to hike from the station to the village. He next pops up at Ashford where he makes a rare visit to the shed. Most of us thrived on outwitting the foremen and getting the numbers before being collared but the collection reveals very few record shots, in this book the only shed visited was Ashford (on three separate occasions!).

(73) V 30934 *St. Lawrence* rests against Ashford's down platform and will go to Ramsgate via Canterbury and Minster. 30934 took a direct hit on the tender from what must have been not the largest of Luftwaffe bombs, because she was sitting on Hungerford Bridge which, too, only suffered repairable damage. *29.5.1959*

(74)   N 31807 is recently ex-works and has been given the new front end for her troubles, less pretty, but they must have considered it worthwhile. *7.5.1961*

Top: (75) Q1 33034 has also come over from the works, and I cannot refuse a shot of a clean one. When they were newish, a driver was courageous/foolish enough to say to Bulleid that they weren't safe at speed, especially tender first - and OVS ordered the driver to uncouple and go flat out down the next bank then he (OVS, dressed in long black coat and homburg) climbed on to the tender and sat with his back to the bunker bulkhead and cried "Right away!" - the driver was determined to have him off and OVS was determined to stay put. Eventually they stopped (and I wish I could remember where this took place) and OVS came down and told the driver, "Nothing wrong with that and don't tell me my engines aren't safe" - I think the driver kept his job but...! *13.5.1961*

Bottom: (76) C 31280 on shed, a couple remained beyond the end of steam to provide the works with steam as required for secular purposes and they were given numbers in the DS Service series. It is interesting, and strange, that he should take but one shot on each call, but maybe he preferred quality to quantity. *22.9.1962*

Opposite: (77) N 31807 leads WC 34012 *Launceston* through Sandling on a down Dover, but where and why was she put on? *27.5.1961*

Top: (78) WC 34101 *Hartland* comes through Sandling Junction station on a down Dover job. It was a long time since this had been "change for Hythe & Sandgate" - for Sandgate had closed to passengers before I was born (the-pre-Cambrian period), and Hythe had gone by 1951 - the station at Hythe was high up and at the back of the town, and the junction at Sandling faced the wrong way; taken all in all, it was a dead duck from square one. *13.5.1961*

(79) BB 34077 *603 Squadron* hops out of the microscopic Sandling Tunnel with a down express but the head code seems wrong for this line although it's not the only shot I know carrying this. *13.5.1961*

(80) N 31807 is framed in the bridge at the west end of Sandling Junction - does that armless post remind us of what was there in 1951? Again, standing off and using the infrastructure is infinitely better than a close-up of a nice clean engine (you can have that in picture 74). *27.5.1961*

Opposite: (81) BB 34071 *601 Squadron* has come up from Dover shed and paused at Folkestone Junction's sub-shed for a drop of water before going across to take on the boat train which has come up the 1 in 30 incline from the harbour - a solitary R1 is visible on what had been the rear of the train; there's probably two or three more jammed against the buffers by Martello Tunnel. *13.4.1961*

Top: (82) BB 34101 *Hartland* is again on the Arrow and in the depths of the Warren where chalk falls were not unknown. The Engineers' Department had a siding here and usually a few empties for loading, they also had their own little toy engine to play with, DS1169, which lived in the open air without protest. *29.5.1961*

Bottom: (83) 30934 *St. Lawrence* leaves Abbotscliffe Tunnel and passes the tiny box used only on busy weekends to break up a longish block. *29.5.1961*

Rear Cover: V 30922 *Marlborough* on a down Hastings near Petts Wood Junction - a familiar location in all conscience, but a different loco and a school which produced two top railwaymen and a top man for the railways - if we speak of John Betjeman firstly it is because one could scarcely imagine a less likely candidate to be their champion, yet he was.

The others were Edward Thompson, Works Manager at Doncaster, subsequently CME of the LNER after Gresley's untimely death, a man whose record is not impeccable, who was either loved or hated for what he did to poor old 4470 *Great Northern*; some ugly and evil-riding Pacifics, yet his rebuilding of J11s, and O4 to either O1 or O4/8 was a wartime masterpiece. Finally, Richard Hardy, a premium apprentice under ET at Doncaster, who always spoke well of him, and became a man-manager such as the railways scarcely knew, who was the Guv'nor at Stewarts Lane in the time when David was taking his first pictures and the source of most of the stories I have recalled - yes, they did happen, it's not just my elderly mind running free.

This has turned out to be more difficult than I expected; finding unpublished pictures for the second half of the book took time, many that I thought were fresh had been skilfully attacked by printers with little external damage to the mounts to give them away - I think the next one will have greater variety of locations for you if not of engines, now being scrapped apace.

Bibliography -

Steam World Magazine 2001 - 2004
A stranger strolls down Stewarts Lane: 40 articles by R.H.N. Hardy
Passengers no more - Ian Allan Publishing.

In the same series...

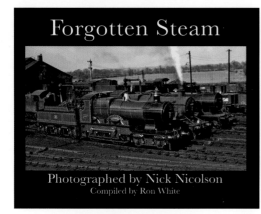

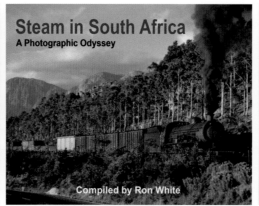

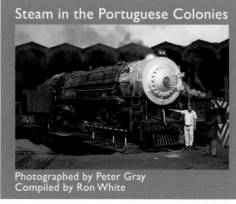

Forgotten Steam
ISBN 978-1-913893-11-8
£16.50

Steam in South Africa
ISBN 978-1-913893-02-6
£16.50

Steam in the Portuguese Colonies
ISBN 978-1-913893-13-2
£16.50

Find us at ttpublishing.co.uk